# The Essential Poets

❖❖

**W9-ACP-240**

FUTURE VOLUMES
WILL INCLUDE

The Essential Donne

The Essential Hopkins

The Essential Hardy

The Essential Wyatt

The Essential Tennyson

The Essential Browning

The Essential Milton

The Essential Marvell

# The Essential Campion

❖

Lord haue mercy vpon mee, O heare my prayrs both

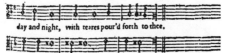

day and night, with teares pour'd forth to thee.

# Thomas Campion

BORN   12 FEBRUARY 1567
DIED    1 MARCH 1620

# The Essential
# CAMPION

Selected and with an
Introduction by
## CHARLES SIMIC

The Ecco Press
New York

*Introduction and selection copyright © 1988 by Charles Simic*
*All rights reserved*
*Published in 1988 by The Ecco Press*
*26 West 17th Street, New York, N.Y. 10011*
*Published simultaneously in Canada by*
*Penguin Books Canada Ltd., Ontario*
*Printed in the United States of America*
*Designed by Reg Perry*
*First Edition*

*Library of Congress Cataloging-in-Publication Data*
*Campion, Thomas, 1567–1620.*
*The essential Campion.*
*(The Essential poets; v. 7)*
*I. Simic, Charles, 1938–     . II. Title.*
*III. Series: Essential poets (New York, N.Y.); v. 7.*
*PR2228.A4   1988   821'.3   88-3736*
*ISBN 0-88001-167-X*
*ISBN 0-88001-172-6 (pbk.)*

*Cover painting: "The Lute Player,"*
*attributed to Caravaggio.*
*Courtesy of the Galleria Sabauda,*
*Torino, Italy.*

*For Anna and Philip*

# Contents

❖❖

# The Essential Campion

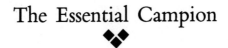

# Introduction

❖❖

He was both poet and musician. The musicians have praised his music and the poets his poetry. Pound and Eliot called him one of the finest lyric poets in the English language. If one defines the lyric as a poem to be sung, he was a master of it. He brought music and poetry together and made us believe they are sister arts, and Orpheus their first great practitioner.

He lived in what was certainly the golden age of these two distinct art forms. Born in 1567, Campion was a contemporary of Shakespeare, Drayton, Marlowe, Nash, and Jonson in literature, and Byrd, Morley, Gibbons, and Dowland in music. "A man of faire parts and good reputation," wrote Samuel Daniel, even while attacking Campion's essay on prosody. There were many such testimonials of his worth during his lifetime.

Ben Jonson is an exception. He knew Campion but offered no praise. Is it possible that the author of "To Celia" was tone-deaf? Jonson complained that "Buchanan (his tutor) had corrupted his ears when young, and learned him to sing verses when he should have read them." That's the view that has prevailed. We no longer sing our poems; we read them to ourselves and rarely aloud.

Campion wrote ayres for solo voice, songs accompanied by a lute. One note to a syllable is how one sets words to music in such a song. The melodies are simple, the words come across distinctly. *Ayre,* of course, implies lightness, airiness. Campion did not care for richness of musical texture. It obscured the text. The same is true of fancy metaphors and conceits. They could not be sung with a straight face.

Today we have Campion's songs on records and can hear what he was after. There was a time, however, a period of almost two hundred years, when even his poems were not available. They lay buried in Elizabethan songbooks, and that kind of music had long gone out of fashion. The great Romantic poets never heard of him. Even Shelley, who equated the poet's psyche with an Aeolian lyre, knew him not. Campion was not rediscovered until the late nineteenth century. Since then, it's been difficult to imagine the history of poetry without him. Whoever dreams of a poem where language begins to resemble music, thinks of him.

Campion's first songs were published in 1601. They appeared in a "Book of Ayres, set foorth to be sung to the lute, Orpherian, and base Violl, by Philip Rosseter, Lutanist." These were not his first published poems. He was known previously as a Latin poet, and had in fact already written a great deal of poetry in that language before turning to songwriting.

It's no wonder that he knew his Latin poets. He attended Peterhouse College, Cambridge, where classical literature was studied seriously. The students rose between four and five in the morning for prayers and were expected to study till ten P.M. Poor Campion didn't even get to go home on vacation. He was an orphan. His father had died when he was nine, and his mother, after remarrying, shortly after. His stepfather and guardian didn't want him around. At Peterhouse, appropriately, like all the other students, he was advised to avoid "finery" and "wear sad colours."

We can assume that Campion participated in the intellectual life of the place. He was, by all accounts, a friendly sort, a man who always had a large circle of friends. His college fostered the study of medicine, and the university itself was famous for its degrees in literary study and music. What we do know is that he left without obtaining a degree, some say because he was a Roman Catholic and Catholics were not allowed to receive one.

Whatever the case may be, we find him next at Gray's Inn in 1586, there, presumably, to study law in the footsteps of his father, a minor law clerk at Chancery Court when he died. Nothing came of it. He participated in masques and revels which were a part of the social activity of the inns of the royal court, and he wrote poetry in Latin. There was obviously a literary circle there, young men showing each other poems and discussing literature.

We know nothing, on the other hand, of Campion's musical education. In 1589 the first book of Italian madrigals appeared in England: Nicholas Young's *Musica Transalpina*. It's well known that at the inns there were many fine musicians and singers. Both the lute song and the madrigal were at the height of their popularity. Campion's interest was both typical of his time and somewhat unusual among poets. He had a single-minded devotion to the lute song.

Campion supported himself during these years by the small inheritance his mother had left him. After the money ran out, he found himself nearing forty and without a profession to support himself. Therefore, in 1602, he enrolled as a medical student at the University of Caen in Normandy, a medical school popular with English students for being close to home, and for being a school that gave quick degrees. Campion received his after three years of study. For the rest of his life he practiced medicine.

The evidence suggests that he was a good doctor, that his reputation was considerable, although he held a degree not recognized by the Royal College of Physicians. The practice did not make him rich. Campion died in 1620 with twenty-two pounds to his name. The money went to his friend and collaborator, Philip Rosseter, so we can assume that he had no close family left.

Campion published quite a bit during his lifetime. In addition to the poems in Latin (*Thomas Campiani Poemata,* 1594) and the first book of ayres we have the important *Observations in the Art of English Poesie* in 1602, *Two Books of Ayres* in 1613(?), *The Third and Fourth Book of Ayres* in 1617(?), several masques, an essay on musical theory, and a final volume of new and revised Latin epigrams, brought out the year before he died.

"What epigrams are in Poetrie, the same are Ayres in musicke," Campion wrote. He made early connection between the two. "Their perfection comes from being short and well-seasoned," he adds. His own poems have the terseness, the wit and bite of a finely wrought epigram.

In *Observations in the Art of English Poesie,* Campion argued for the superiority of classical prosody over the English practice. He prefers the Latin poet's measuring the length of the syllables to the native poet's reliance on stress alone. He understands the difficulty of applying Latin prosody to "our toonge," asks only that closer attention be paid to syllable length so that the measure may be more precise.

The underlying issue is, obviously, the setting of words to music. He says: "In joyning words to harmony there is nothing more offensive to the eare than to place a long sillable with a short note, or short sillable with a long note, though in the last the vowell often beares it out."

His other complaint is rhyme—that "Medieval barbarism," he calls it! The attention it receives is at the expense of the integrity of the individual line of poetry. Campion gives examples of rhyme used to conceal the defects of the line. For him the line is all-important. As

Robert Creeley says, "The line is the means to focus, is that which says 'how' we are to weight *things* we are told. And as it is there, to do this work, so the words break through their *sense*"—and their song, Campion might have added.

"What musick can there be where there's no proportion observed?" he writes. "The eare is a rational sence and a chief judge of proportion." As the musician fine-tunes his instrument, so the poet tunes the lines of his poem.

Leibnitz had the idea that "unconscious mathematical operations of the soul are the basis of our enjoyment of music," and Campion would have agreed. This is the religion of the lyric poet. "All inmost things are melodious," said Carlyle. Music is the way the self finds a relationship to something beyond itself, "the bridge between consciousness and the unthinking sentient or even insentient universe," in Pound's words.

"The world is made by Simmetry and proportion, and is in that respect compared to Musick, and Musick to Poetry," was Campion's view. The cosmology of the lute song is Pythagorean. As above so below. "Tune thy music to the heart," as our poet said.

Economy is both an ideal and a practical necessity for Campion. This is a poetry with a minimum of imagery and little ornamentation; pithy as the epigram. Adjectives are avoided and so are abstractions. There are a good many conventional phrases, well-worn Petrarchan echoings. The subject, in short, is familiar; all invention is concentrated on the treatment.

Campion's poems, despite their literary allusions, have something of folk songs about them. In both, understatement is the rule. What is known in rhetoric as paralipsis: the suggestion by the deliberately concise treatment of a topic that much of significance is being omitted, but is nevertheless implied. This is especially true of Campion's later poems where the psychology of the speaker begins to play a greater role. He or she may say one thing, but we know there's more to it.

As always, the subject matter of these poems is the tragicomedy of courtship, matrimony, adultery, sexuality—in other words, the eternal human predicament: Truths which are also clichés which are also eternal human truths. Campion has been called "Platonically cold," but he's really a tough-minded realist.

If there's one theme that seems to run through many poems, it is that of seduction. "Born of literature, able to speak only with the help of worn codes" (Barthes), the act itself and its tragicomedy is entirely a matter of language. Campion's lovers yearn to fall under the spell of words, but somehow they're unable to. They're constantly looking over their shoulders and eavesdropping on themselves. The sublime-turning-into-ridiculous is their lot.

Campion's poems are printed here without his music as is now mostly the case. With most songwriters this would be disastrous. The music is usually—and it is—an integral part of the whole. For example, only a few of the most heartbreaking blues song texts can stand alone as poems. Campion is an exception. His lyrics are some of the best poems in the language.

If ever poetry needed to be read aloud, his ought to be. The phrase "auditory imagination" begins to acquire meaning then. The ancients used to make a distinction between truth that is seen and truth that is heard. Every great lyric poem recapitulates the whole history of listening to the mother tongue.

— CHARLES SIMIC

# Poems

♦ ♦ ♦ ♦ ♦

My sweetest Lesbia, let us live and love,
And, though the sager sort our deedes reprove,
Let us not way them: heav'ns great lampes doe dive
Into their west, and strait againe revive,
But, soone as once set is our little light,
Then must we sleepe one ever-during night.

If all would lead their lives in love like mee,
Then bloudie swords and armour should not be,
No drum nor trumpet peaceful sleepes should move,
Unles alar'me came from the campe of love:
But fooles do live, and wast their little light,
And seeke with paine their ever-during night.

When timely death my life and fortune ends,
Let not my hearse be vext with mourning friends,
But let all lovers, rich in triumph, come,
And with sweet pastimes grace my happie tombe;
And, Lesbia, close up thou my little light,
And crowne with love my ever-during night.

♦ ♦ ♦ ♦ ♦

Though you are yoong and I am olde,
Though your vaines hot and my bloud colde,
Though youth is moist and age is drie,
Yet embers live when flames doe die.

The tender graft is easely broke,
But who shall shake the sturdie Oke?
You are more fresh and faire then I,
Yet stubs doe live, when flowers doe die.

Thou that thy youth doest vainely boast,
Know buds are soonest nipt with frost;
Thinke that thy fortune still doth crie,
Thou foole, tomorrow thou must die.

♦ ♦ ♦ ♦ ♦

I care not for these Ladies
That must be woode and praide,
Give me kind Amarillis
The wanton countrey maide;
Nature art disdaineth,
Her beautie is her owne;
    Her when we court and kisse,
    She cries, forsooth, let go:
    But when we come where comfort is,
    She never will say no.

If I love Amarillis,
She gives me fruit and flowers,
But if we love these Ladies,

We must give golden showers;
Give them gold that sell love,
Give me the Nutbrowne lasse,
>    Who when we court and kisse,
>    She cries, forsooth, let go:
>    But when we come where comfort is,
>    She never will say no.

These Ladies must have pillowes,
And beds by strangers wrought,
Give me a Bower of willowes,
Of mosse and leaves unbought,
And fresh Amarillis,
With milke and honie fed,
>    Who when we court and kisse,
>    She cries, forsooth, let go:
>    But when we come where comfort is,
>    She never will say no.

◆ ◆ ◆ ◆ ◆

Followe thy faire sunne, unhappy shaddowe:
Though thou be blacke as night,
And she made all of light,
Yet follow thy faire sunne, unhappie shaddowe.

Follow her whose light thy light depriveth:
Though here thou liv'st disgrac't,
And she in heaven is plac't,
Yet follow her whose light the world reviveth.

Follow those pure beames whose beautie burneth,
That so have scorched thee,

As thou still blacke must bee,
Til her kind beames thy black to brightnes turneth.

Follow her while yet her glorie shineth:
There comes a luckles night,
That will dim all her light;
And this the black unhappie shade devineth.

Follow still since so thy fates ordained:
The Sunne must have his shade,
Till both at once doe fade,
The Sun still prov'd, the shadow still disdained.

♦ ♦ ♦ ♦ ♦

When to her lute Corrina sings,
Her voice revives the leaden stringes,
And doth in highest noates appeare
As any challeng'd eccho cleere;
But when she doth of mourning speake,
Ev'n with her sighes the strings do breake.

And, as her lute doth live or die,
Led by her passion, so must I:
For when of pleasure she doth sing,
My thoughts enjoy a sodaine spring;
But if she doth of sorrow speake,
Ev'n from my hart the strings doe breake.

♦ ♦ ♦ ♦ ♦

My love hath vowd hee will forsake mee,
And I am alreadie sped.
Far other promise he did make me
When he had my maidenhead.
If such danger be in playing,
And sport must to earnest turne,
I will go no more a-maying.

Had I foreseene what is ensued,
And what now with paine I prove,
Unhappie then I had eschewed
This unkind event of love:
Maides foreknow their own undooing,
But feare naught till all is done,
When a man alone is wooing.

Dissembling wretch, to gaine thy pleasure,
What didst thou not vow and sweare?
So didst thou rob me of the treasure
Which so long I held so deare;
Now thou prov'st to me a stranger,
Such is the vile guise of men
When a woman is in danger.

That hart is neerest to misfortune
That will trust a fained toong;
When flattring men our loves importune,
They entend us deepest wrong;
If this shame of loves betraying
But this once I cleanely shun,
I will go no more a-maying.

◆ ◆ ◆ ◆ ◆

Turne backe, you wanton flyer,
And answere my desire
With mutuall greeting;
Yet bende a little neerer,
True beauty stil shines cleerer
In closer meeting.
Harts with harts delighted
Should strive to be united,
Either others armes with armes enchayning:
Harts with a thought, rosie lips
With a kisse still entertaining.

What harvest halfe so sweete is
As still to reape the kisses
Growne ripe in sowing,
And straight to be receiver
Of that which thou art giver,
Rich in bestowing?
There's no strickt observing
Of times, or seasons changing,
There is ever one fresh spring abiding:
Then what we sow with our lips
Let us reape, loves gaines deviding.

◆ ◆ ◆ ◆ ◆

The Sypres curten of the night is spread,
And over all a silent dewe is cast.
The weaker cares by sleepe are conquered;
But I alone, with hidious griefe agast,

In spite of Morpheus charmes a watch doe keepe
Over mine eies, to banish carelesse sleepe.

Yet oft my trembling eyes through faintnes close,
And then the Mappe of hell before me stands,
Which Ghosts doe see, and I am one of those
Ordain'd to pine in sorrowes endles bands,
Since from my wretched soule all hopes are reft
And now no cause of life to me is left.

Griefe, ceaze my soule, for that will still endure
When my cras'd bodie is consum'd and gone;
Beare it to thy blacke denne, there keepe it sure,
Where thou ten thousand soules doest tyre upon:
Yet all doe not affoord such foode to thee
As this poore one, the worser part of mee.

♦ ♦ ♦ ♦ ♦

Follow your Saint, follow with accents sweet,
Haste you, sad noates, fall at her flying feete;
There, wrapt in cloud of sorrowe, pitie move,
And tell the ravisher of my soule I perish for her love.
But if she scorns my never-ceasing paine,
Then burst with sighing in her sight, and nere returne againe.

All that I soong still to her praise did tend,
Still she was first, still she my songs did end.
Yet she my love and Musicke both doeth flie,
The Musicke that her Eccho is, and beauties simpathie;
Then let my Noates pursue her scornefull flight:
It shall suffice that they were breath'd, and dyed, for her delight.

♦ ♦ ♦ ♦ ♦

It fell on a sommers day,
While sweete Bessie sleeping laie
In her bowre, on her bed,
Light with curtaines shadowed;
Jamy came, shee him spies,
Opning halfe her heavie eies.

Jamy stole in through the dore,
She lay slumbring as before;
Softly to her he drew neere,
She heard him, yet would not heare;
Bessie vow'd not to speake,
He resolv'd that dumpe to breake.

First a soft kisse he doth take,
She lay still, and would not wake;
Then his hands learn'd to woo,
She dreamp't not what he would doo,
But still slept, while he smild
To see love by sleepe beguild.

Jamy then began to play,
Bessie as one buried lay,
Gladly still through this sleight
Deceiv'd in her owne deceit;
And, since this traunce begoon,
She sleepes ev'rie afternoone.

♦ ♦ ♦ ♦ ♦

Thou art not faire, for all thy red and white,
For all those rosie ornaments in thee;
Thou art not sweet, though made of meer delight,
Nor faire nor sweet, unlesse thou pitie mee.
I will not sooth thy fancies: thou shalt prove
That beauty is no beautie without love.

Yet love not me, nor seeke thou to allure
My thoughts with beautie, were it more devine;
Thy smiles and kisses I cannot endure,
I'le not be wrapt up in those armes of thine.
Now shew it, if thou be a woman right:
Embrace, and kisse, and love me, in despight.

♦ ♦ ♦ ♦ ♦

See where she flies enrag'd from me,
View her when she intends despite:
The winde is not more swift then shee,
Her furie mov'd such terror makes
As, to a fearfull guiltie sprite,
The voice of heav'ns huge thunder cracks.
But, when her appeased minde yeelds to delight,
All her thoughts are made of joyes,
Millions of delights inventing:
Other pleasures are but toies
To her beauties sweete contenting.

My fortune hangs upon her brow,
For, as she smiles or frownes on mee,
So must my blowne affections bow;

And her proude thoughts too well do find
With what unequall tyrannie
Her beauties doe command my mind.
Though, when her sad planet raignes, froward she bee,
She alone can pleasure move,
And displeasing sorrow banish:
May I but still hold her love,
Let all other comforts vanish.

♦ ♦ ♦ ♦ ♦

Blame not my cheeks, though pale with love they be;
The kindly heate unto my heart is flowne,
To cherish it that is dismaid by thee,
Who art so cruell and unsteedfast growne:
For nature, cald for by distressed harts,
Neglects and quite forsakes the outward partes.

But they whose cheekes with careles blood are stain'd
Nurse not one sparke of love within their harts,
And, when they woe, they speake with passion fain'd,
For their fat love lyes in their outward parts:
But in their brests, where love his court should hold,
Poore Cupid sits and blowes his nailes for cold.

♦ ♦ ♦ ♦ ♦

When the God of merrie love
As yet in his cradle lay,
Thus his wither'd nurse did say:
Thou a wanton boy wilt prove
To deceive the powers above;

For by thy continuall smiling
I see thy power of beguiling.

Therewith she the babe did kisse,
When a sodaine fire out came
From those burning lips of his,
That did her with love enflame;
But none would regard the same,
So that, to her daie of dying,
The old wretch liv'd ever crying.

♦ ♦ ♦ ♦ ♦

Your faire lookes enflame my desire:
    Quench it againe with love.
Stay, O strive not still to retire,
    Doe not inhumane prove.
If love may perswade,
    Loves pleasures, deere, denie not;
Heere is a silent grovie shade:
    O tarrie then, and flie not.

Have I seaz'd my heavenly delight
    In this unhaunted grove?
Time shall now her furie requite
    With the revenge of love.
Then come, sweetest, come,
    My lips with kisses gracing:
Here let us harbour all alone,
    Die, die in sweete embracing.

Will you now so timely depart,
    And not returne againe?

Your sight lends such life to my hart
    That to depart is paine.
Feare yeelds no delay,
    Securenes helpeth pleasure:
Then, till the time gives safer stay,
    O farewell, my lives treasure!

♦ ♦ ♦ ♦ ♦

The man of life upright,
    Whose guiltlesse hart is free
From all dishonest deedes,
    Or thought of vanitie,

The man whose silent dayes
    In harmeles joyes are spent,
Whome hopes cannot delude,
    Nor sorrow discontent,

That man needes neither towers
    Nor armour for defence,
Nor secret vautes to flie
    From thunders violence.

Hee onely can behold
    With unafrighted eyes
The horrours of the deepe,
    And terrours of the Skies.

Thus, scorning all the cares
    That fate, or fortune brings,
He makes the heav'n his booke,
    His wisedome heev'nly things,

Good thoughts his onely friendes,
   His wealth a well-spent age,
The earth his sober Inne,
   And quiet Pilgrimage.

◆ ◆ ◆ ◆ ◆

Harke, al you ladies that do sleep:
   the fayry queen Proserpina
Bids you awake and pitie them that weep;
   you may doe in the darke
What the day doth forbid:
   feare not the dogs that barke,
      Night will have all hid.

But if you let your lovers mone,
   the Fairie Queene Proserpina
Will send abroad her Fairies ev'rie one,
   that shall pinch blacke and blew
Your white hands, and faire armes,
   that did not kindly rue
      Your Paramours harmes.

In Myrtle Arbours on the downes,
   the Fairie Queene Proserpina,
This night by moone-shine leading merrie rounds,
   holds a watch with sweet love;
Downe the dale, up the hill,
   no plaints or groanes may move
      Their holy vigill.

All you that will hold watch with love,
   the Fairie Queene Proserpina

Will make you fairer then Diones dove;
   Roses red, Lillies white,
And the cleare damaske hue,
   shall on your cheekes alight:
      Love will adorne you.

All you that love, or lov'd before,
   the Fairie Queene Proserpina
Bids you encrease that loving humour more:
   they that yet have not fed
On delight amorous,
   she vowes that they shall lead
      Apes in Avernus.

◆ ◆ ◆ ◆ ◆

When thou must home to shades of under ground,
And there ariv'd, a newe admired guest,
The beauteous spirits do ingirt thee round,
White Iope, blith Hellen, and the rest,
To heare the stories of thy finisht love,
From that smoothe toong whose musicke hell can move:

Then wilt thou speake of banqueting delights,
Of masks and revels which sweete youth did make,
Of Turnies and great challenges of knights,
And all these triumphes for thy beauties sake:
When thou hast told these honours done to thee,
Then tell, O tell, how thou didst murther me.

♦ ♦ ♦ ♦ ♦

Where are all thy beauties now, all harts enchayning?
Whither are thy flatt'rers gone with all their fayning?
All fled; and thou alone still here remayning.

Thy rich state of twisted gold to Bayes is turned;
Cold as thou art, are thy loves that so much burned:
Who dye in flatt'rers armes are seldome mourned.

Yet, in spight of envie, this be still proclaymed,
That none worthyer then thy selfe thy worth hath blamed:
When their poore names are lost, thou shalt live famed.

When thy story, long time hence, shall be perused,
Let the blemish of thy rule be thus excused:
None ever liv'd more just, none more abused.


♦ ♦ ♦ ♦ ♦

Out of my soules deapth to thee my cryes have sounded:
Let thine eares my plaints receive, on just feare grounded.
Lord, should'st thou weigh our faults, who's not confounded?

But with grace thou censur'st thine when they have erred,
Therefore shall thy blessed name be lov'd and feared:
Ev'n to thy throne my thoughts and eyes are reared.

Thee alone my hopes attend, on thee relying;
In thy sacred word I'le trust, to thee fast flying,
Long ere the Watch shall breake, the morne descrying.

In the mercies of our God who live secured,
May of full redemption rest in him assured;
Their sinne-sicke soules by him shall be recured.


◆ ◆ ◆ ◆ ◆


Bravely deckt, come forth, bright day,
Thine houres with Roses strew thy way,
    As they well remember.
Thou receiv'd shalt be with feasts:
Come, chiefest of the *British* ghests,
    Thou fift of *November.*
Thou with triumph shalt exceede
    In the strictest ember;
For by thy returne the Lord records his blessed deede.


*Britaines,* frolicke at your bourd,
But first sing praises to the Lord
    In your Congregations.
Hee preserv'd your state alone,
His loving grace hath made you one
    Of his chosen Nations.
But this light must hallowed be
    With your best Oblations;
Prayse the Lord, for onely great and mercifull is hee.


Death had enter'd in the gate,
And ruine was crept neare the State;
    But heav'n all revealed.
Fi'ry Powder hell did make,
Which, ready long the flame to take,
    Lay in shade concealed.
God us helpt of his free grace,

None to him appealed;
For none was so bad to feare the treason or the place.

God his peacefull Monarch chose,
To him the mist he did disclose,
        To him, and none other;
This hee did, O King, for thee,
That thou thine owne renowne might'st see,
        Which no time can smother.
May blest *Charles* thy comfort be,
        Firmer then his Brother:
May his heart the love of peace, and wisedome learne
        from thee.


◆ ◆ ◆ ◆ ◆


Tune thy Musicke to thy hart,
Sing thy joy with thankes, and so thy sorrow:
        Though Devotion needes not Art,
Sometime of the poore the rich may borrow.

Strive not yet for curious wayes:
Concord pleaseth more, the lesse 'tis strained;
        Zeale affects not outward prayse,
Onely strives to shew a love unfained.

Love can wondrous things effect,
Sweetest Sacrifice, all wrath appeasing;
        Love the highest doth respect,
Love alone to him is ever pleasing.

♦ ♦ ♦ ♦ ♦

Most sweet and pleasing are thy wayes, O God,
Like Meadowes deckt with Christall streames and flowers:
Thy paths no foote prophane hath ever trod,
Nor hath the proud man rested in thy Bowers.
There lives no Vultur, no devouring Beare,
But onely Doves and Lambs are harbor'd there.

The Wolfe his young ones to their prey doth guide;
The Foxe his Cubbs with false deceit endues;
The Lyons Whelpe suckes from his Damme his pride;
In hers the Serpent malice doth infuse:
The darksome Desart all such beasts contaynes,
Not one of them in Paradice remaynes.

♦ ♦ ♦ ♦ ♦

Never weather-beaten Saile more willing bent to shore,
Never tyred Pilgrims limbs affected slumber more,
Then my weary spright now longs to flye out of my troubled brest.
    O come quickly, sweetest Lord, and take my soule to rest.

Ever-blooming are the joyes of Heav'ns high paradice,
Cold age deafes not there our eares, nor vapour dims our eyes;
Glory there the Sun outshines, whose beames the blessed onely see:
    O come quickly, glorious Lord, and raise my spright to thee.

♦ ♦ ♦ ♦ ♦

Loe, when backe mine eye,
   Pilgrim-like, I cast,
What fearefull wayes I spye,
Which, blinded, I securely past!

But now heav'n hath drawne
   From my browes that night;
As when the day doth dawne,
So cleares my long imprison'd sight.

Straight the caves of hell
   Drest with flowres I see,
Wherein false pleasures dwell,
That, winning most, most deadly be.

Throngs of masked Feinds,
   Wing'd like Angels, flye,
Ev'n in the gates of Friends;
In faire disguise blacke dangers lye.

Straight to Heav'n I rais'd
   My restored sight,
And with loud voyce I prais'd
The Lord of ever-during light.

And, since I had stray'd
   From his wayes so wide,
His grace I humbly pray'd
Hence-forth to be my guard and guide.

◆ ◆ ◆ ◆ ◆

As by the streames of *Babilon,*
Farre from our native soyle we sat,
Sweet *Sion,* thee we thought upon,
And ev'ry thought a teare begat.

Aloft the trees that spring up there
Our silent Harps wee pensive hung:
Said they that captiv'd us, Let's heare
Some song which you in *Sion* sung.

Is then the song of our God fit
To be prophan'd in forraine land?
O *Salem,* thee when I forget,
Forget his skill may my right hand!

Fast to the roofe cleave may my tongue,
If mindelesse I of thee be found:
Or if, when all my joyes are sung,
*Jerusalem* be not the ground.

Remember, Lord, how *Edoms* race
Cryed in *Jerusalems* sad day,
Hurle downe her wals, her towres deface;
And, stone by stone, all levell lay.

Curst *Babels* seede! for *Salems* sake
Just ruine yet for thee remaines!
Blest shall they be, thy babes that take,
And 'gainst the stones dash out their braines!

♦ ♦ ♦ ♦ ♦

Come, chearfull day, part of my life, to mee:
For, while thou view'st me with thy fading light,
Part of my life doth still depart with thee,
And I still onward haste to my last night.
  Times fatall wings doe ever forward flye,
  Soe ev'ry day we live, a day wee dye.

But, O yee nights ordain'd for barren rest,
How are my dayes depriv'd of life in you,
When heavy sleepe my soule hath dispossest,
By fayned death life sweetly to renew!
  Part of my life, in that, you life denye:
  So ev'ry day we live, a day wee dye.


♦ ♦ ♦ ♦ ♦

*Jacke* and *Jone,* they thinke no ill,
  But loving live, and merry still;
  Doe their weeke dayes worke, and pray
  Devotely on the holy day;
  Skip and trip it on the greene,
  And help to chuse the Summer Queene;
  Lash out, at a Country Feast,
  Their silver penny with the best.

Well can they judge of nappy Ale,
  And tell at large a Winter tale;
  Climbe up to the Apple loft,
  And turne the Crabs till they be soft.
*Tib* is all the fathers joy,
  And little *Tom* the mothers boy.

All their pleasure is content;
And care, to pay their yearely rent.

*Jone* can call by name her Cowes,
And decke her windowes with greene boughs;
Shee can wreathes and tuttyes make,
And trimme with plums a Bridall Cake.
*Jacke* knowes what brings gaine or losse,
And his long Flaile can stoutly tosse;
Make the hedge, which others breake,
And ever thinkes what he doth speake.

Now, you Courtly Dames and Knights,
That study onely strange delights,
Though you scorne the home-spun gray,
And revell in your rich array;
Though your tongues dissemble deepe,
And can your heads from danger keepe;
Yet, for all your pompe and traine,
Securer lives the silly Swaine.

♦ ♦ ♦ ♦ ♦

All lookes be pale, harts cold as stone.
For *Hally* now is dead, and gone,
    *Hally,* in whose sight,
      Most sweet sight,
        All the earth late tooke delight.
  Ev'ry eye, weepe with mee,
  Joyes drown'd in teares must be.

His Iv'ry skin, his comely hayre,
His Rosie cheekes, so cleare and faire,

Eyes that once did grace
      His bright face,
   Now in him all want their place.
Eyes and hearts, weepe with mee,
For who so kinde as hee?

His youth was like an *Aprill* flowre,
Adorn'd with beauty, love, and powre;
      Glory strow'd his way,
         Whose wreaths gay
      Now are all turn'd to decay.
Then againe weepe with mee,
None feele more cause then wee.

No more may his wisht sight returne,
His golden Lampe no more can burne;
      Quencht is all his flame,
         His hop't fame
      Now hath left him nought but name.
For him all weepe with mee,
Since more him none shall see.

♦ ♦ ♦ ♦ ♦

Vaine men, whose follies make a God of Love,
Whose blindnesse beauty doth immortall deeme:
Prayse not what you desire, but what you prove,
Count those things good that are, not those that seeme:
I cannot call her true that's false to me,
Nor make of women more then women be.

How faire an entrance breakes the way to love!
How rich of golden hope, and gay delight!

What hart cannot a modest beauty move?
Who, seeing cleare day once, will dreame of night?
Shee seem'd a Saint, that brake her faith with mee,
But prov'd a woman, as all other be.

So bitter is their sweet, that true content
Unhappy men in them may never finde;
Ah, but without them, none; both must consent,
Else uncouth are the joyes of eyther kinde.
Let us then prayse their good, forget their ill:
Men must be men, and women women still.

◆ ◆ ◆ ◆ ◆

How eas'ly wert thou chained,
Fond hart, by favours fained!
Why liv'd thy hopes in grace,
Straight to dye disdained?
But, since th' art now beguiled
By Love that falsely smiled,
In some lesse happy place
Mourne alone exiled.
My love still here increaseth,
And with my love my griefe,
While her sweet bounty ceaseth,
That gave my woes reliefe.
Yet 'tis no woman leaves me,
For such may prove unjust:
A Goddesse thus deceives me,
Whose faith who could mistrust?

A Goddesse so much graced
That Paradice is placed

In her most heav'nly brest,
Once by love embraced;
But love, that so kinde proved,
Is now from her removed,
Nor will he longer rest
Where no faith is loved.
If Powres Celestiall wound us
And will not yeeld reliefe,
Woe then must needs confound us,
For none can cure our griefe.
No wonder if I languish
Through burden of my smart;
It is no common anguish
From Paradice to part.

♦ ♦ ♦ ♦ ♦

O what unhop't for sweet supply!
　O what joyes exceeding!
What an affecting charme feele I,
　From delight proceeding!
That which I long despair'd to be,
　To her I am, and shee to mee.

Shee that alone in cloudy griefe
　Long to mee appeared,
Shee now alone with bright reliefe
　All those clouds hath cleared.
Both are immortall, and divine,
　Since I am hers, and she is mine.

♦ ♦ ♦ ♦ ♦

Where shee her sacred bowre adornes,
   The Rivers clearly flow:
The groves and medowes swell with flowres,
   The windes all gently blow:
Her Sunne-like beauty shines so fayre,
   Her Spring can never fade:
Who then can blame the life that strives
   To harbour in her shade?

Her grace I sought, her love I wooed;
   Her love though I obtaine,
No time, no toyle, no vow, no faith
   Her wished grace can gaine.
Yet truth can tell my heart is hers,
   And her will I adore:
And from that love when I depart,
 · Let heav'n view me no more.

Her roses with my prayer shall spring;
   And when her trees I praise,
Their boughs shall blossome, mellow fruit
   Shall straw her pleasant wayes.
The words of harty zeale have powre
   High wonders to effect;
O why should then her Princely eare
   My words, or zeale neglect?

If shee my faith misdeemes, or worth,
   Woe-worth my haplesse fate:
For, though time can my truth reveale,
   That time will come too late.
And who can glory in the worth

That cannot yeeld him grace?
Content in ev'ry thing is not,
   Nor joy in ev'ry place.

But, from her bowre of Joy since I
   Must now excluded be,
And shee will not relieve my cares,
   Which none can helpe but shee:
My comfort in her love shall dwell,
   Her love lodge in my brest;
And though not in her bowre, yet I
   Shall in her temple rest.

◆ ◆ ◆ ◆ ◆

Faine would I my love disclose,
Aske what honour might denye;
But both love and her I lose,
From my motion if shee flye.
Worse then paine is feare to mee:
Then hold in fancy, though it burne;
If not happy, safe Ile be,
And to my clostred cares returne.

Yet, o yet, in vaine I strive
To represse my school'd desire;
More and more the flames revive,
I consume in mine owne fire.
She would pitty, might shee know
The harmes that I for her endure:
Speake then, and get comfort so:
A wound long hid growes past recure.

Wise shee is, and needs must know
All th' attempts that beauty moves:
Fayre she is, and honour'd so
That she, sure, hath tryed some loves.
If with love I tempt her then,
'Tis but her due to be desir'd:
What would women thinke of men,
If their deserts were not admir'd?

Women, courted, have the hand
To discard what they distaste:
But those Dames whom none demand
Want oft what their wils imbrac't.
Could their firmnesse iron excell,
As they are faire, they should be sought:
When true theeves use falsehood well,
As they are wise, they will be caught.

♦ ♦ ♦ ♦ ♦

O deare, that I with thee might live,
    From humane trace removed:
Where jealous care might neither grieve,
    Yet each dote on their loved.
While fond feare may colour finde, Love's seldome pleased;
But much like a sicke mans rest, it's soone diseased.

Why should our mindes not mingle so,
    When love and faith is plighted,
That eyther might the others know,
    Alike in all delighted?
Why should frailtie breed suspect, when hearts are fixed?
Must all humane joyes of force with griefe be mixed?

How oft have wee ev'n smilde in teares,
    Our fond mistrust repenting?
As snow when heav'nly fire appeares,
    So melts loves hate relenting.
Vexed kindnesse soone fals off, and soone returneth:
Such a flame the more you quench, the more it burneth.

♦ ♦ ♦ ♦ ♦

Good men, shew, if you can tell,
Where doth humane pittie dwell?
Farre and neere her would I seeke,
So vext with sorrow is my brest.
She (they say) to all is meeke,
And onely makes th' unhappie blest.

Oh! if such a Saint there be,
Some hope yet remaines for me:
Prayer or sacrifice may gaine
From her implored grace reliefe,
To release mee of my paine,
Or at the least to ease my griefe.

Young am I, and farre from guile;
The more is my woe the while:
Falshood with a smooth disguise
My simple meaning hath abus'd,
Casting mists before mine eyes,
By which my senses are confus'd.

Faire he is, who vow'd to me
That he onely mine would be:
But, alas, his minde is caught

With ev'ry gaudie bait he sees.
And too late my flame is taught
That too much kindnesse makes men freese.

From me all my friends are gone,
While I pine for him alone;
And not one will rue my case,
But rather my distresse deride:
That I thinke there is no place
Where pittie ever yet did bide.

♦ ♦ ♦ ♦ ♦

What harvest halfe so sweet is,
As still to reape the kisses
   Growne ripe in sowing?
And straight to be receiver
Of that which thou art giver,
   Rich in bestowing?
Kisse then, my harvest Queene,
   Full garners heaping;
Kisses, ripest when th' are greene,
   Want onely reaping.

The Dove alone expresses
Her fervencie in kisses,
   Of all most loving:
A creature as offencelesse
As those things that are sencelesse
   And void of moving.
Let us so love and kisse,
   Though all envie us:

That which kinde, and harmelesse is,
    None can denie us.


◆ ◆ ◆ ◆ ◆


Sweet, exclude mee not, nor be divided
    From him that ere long must bed thee:
All thy maiden doubts Law hath decided;
    Sure wee are, and I must wed thee.
    Presume then yet a little more:
      Here's the way, barre not the dore.

Tenants, to fulfill their Land-lords pleasure,
    Pay their rent before the quarter:
'Tis my case, if you it rightly measure;
    Put mee not then off with laughter.
    Consider then a little more:
      Here's the way to all my store.

Why were dores in loves despight devised?
    Are not Lawes enough restrayning?
Women are most apt to be surprised
    Sleeping, or sleepe wisely fayning.
    Then grace me yet a little more:
      Here's the way, barre not the dore.


◆ ◆ ◆ ◆ ◆


The peacefull westerne winde
The winter stormes hath tam'd,
And nature in each kinde
The kinde heat hath inflam'd.

The forward buds so sweetly breathe
　　Out of their earthy bowers,
That heav'n, which viewes their pompe beneath,
　　Would faine be deckt with flowers.

　　　See how the morning smiles
　　　On her bright easterne hill,
　　　And with soft steps beguiles
　　　Them that lie slumbring still.
The musicke-loving birds are come
　　From cliffes and rockes unknowne,
To see the trees and briers blome
　　That late were over-flowne.

　　　What Saturne did destroy,
　　　Loves Queene revives againe;
　　　And now her naked boy
　　　Doth in the fields remaine:
Where he such pleasing change doth view
　　In ev'ry living thing,
As if the world were borne anew
　　To gratifie the Spring.

　　　If all things life present,
　　　Why die my comforts then?
　　　Why suffers my content?
　　　Am I the worst of men?
O beautie, be not thou accus'd
　　Too justly in this case:
Unkindly if true love be us'd,
　　'Twill yeeld thee little grace.

♦ ♦ ♦ ♦ ♦

There is none, O none but you,
    That from mee estrange your sight,
Whom mine eyes affect to view
    Or chained eares heare with delight.

Other beauties others move,
    In you I all graces finde:
Such is the effect of love,
    To make them happy that are kinde.

Women in fraile beauty trust,
    Onely seeme you faire to mee;
Yet prove truely kinde and just,
    For that may not dissembled be.

Sweet, afford mee then your sight,
    That, survaying all your lookes,
Endlesse volumes I may write,
    And fill the world with envyed bookes:

Which when after ages view,
    All shall wonder, and despaire,
Woman to finde man so true,
    Or man a woman halfe so faire.

♦ ♦ ♦ ♦ ♦

Pin'd I am, and like to die,
And all for lacke of that which I
    Doe ev'ry day refuse.
If I musing sit, or stand,

Some puts it daily in my hand,
    To interrupt my muse.
The same thing I seeke, and flie,
And want that which none would denie.

In my bed, when I should rest,
It breeds such trouble in my brest
    That scarce mine eyes will close:
If I sleepe, it seemes to be
Oft playing in the bed with me,
    But, wak't, away it goes.
Tis some spirit, sure, I weene,
And yet it may be felt, and seene.

Would I had the heart and wit
To make it stand, and conjure it,
    That haunts me thus with feare.
Doubtlesse tis some harmlesse spright,
For it by day, as well as night,
    Is ready to appeare.
Be it friend, or be it foe,
Ere long Ile trie what it will doe.


◆ ◆ ◆ ◆ ◆


So many loves have I neglected
    Whose good parts might move mee,
That now I live of all rejected,
    There is none will love me.
Why is mayden heate so coy?
    It freezeth when it burneth,
Looseth what it might injoy,
    And, having lost it, mourneth.

Should I then wooe, that have been wooed,
    Seeking them that flye mee?
When I my faith with teares have vowed,
    And when all denye mee,
Who will pitty my disgrace,
    Which love might have prevented?
There is no submission base
    Where error is repented.

O happy men, whose hopes are licenc'd
    To discourse their passion,
While women are confin'd to silence,
    Loosing wisht occasion.
Yet our tongues then theirs, men say,
    Are apter to be moving:
Women are more dumbe then they,
    But in their thoughts more roving.

When I compare my former strangenesse
    With my present doting,
I pitty men that speake in plainenesse,
    Their true hearts devoting;
While wee with repentance jest
    At their submissive passion:
Maydes, I see, are never blest
    That strange be but for fashion.

◆ ◆ ◆ ◆ ◆

Though your strangenesse frets my hart,
Yet may not I complaine:
You perswade me, 'tis but Art,
That secret love must faine.

If another you affect,
'Tis but a shew t' avoid suspect.
Is this faire excusing? O no, all is abusing.

Your wisht sight if I desire,
Suspitions you pretend;
Causelesse you your selfe retire,
While I in vaine attend.
This a Lover whets, you say,
Still made more eager by delay.
Is this faire excusing? O no, all is abusing.

When another holds your hand,
You sweare I hold your hart:
When my Rivals close doe stand
And I sit farre apart,
I am neerer yet then they,
Hid in your bosome, as you say.
Is this faire excusing? O no, all is abusing.

Would my Rival then I were,
Some els your secret friend:
So much lesser should I feare,
And not so much attend.
They enjoy you, ev'ry one,
Yet I must seeme your friend alone.
Is this faire excusing? O no, all is abusing.

♦ ♦ ♦ ♦ ♦

Come away, arm'd with loves delights,
    Thy sprightfull graces bring with thee:
When loves longing fights,

They must the sticklers be.
Come quickly, come, the promis'd houre is wel-nye spent,
And pleasure, being too much deferr'd, looseth her best content.

Is shee come? O, how neare is shee?
How farre yet from this friendly place?
How many steps from me?
When shall I her imbrace?
These armes Ile spred, which onely at her sight shall close,
Attending as the starry flowre that the Suns noone-tide knowes.

◆ ◆ ◆ ◆ ◆

Come, you pretty false-ey'd wanton,
Leave your crafty smiling:
Thinke you to escape me now
With slipp'ry words beguiling?
No; you mock't me th' other day,
When you got loose, you fled away;
But, since I have caught you now,
Ile clip your wings for flying:
Smothring kisses fast Ile heape,
And keepe you so from crying.

Sooner may you count the starres,
And number hayle downe pouring,
Tell the Osiers of the *Temmes,*
Or *Goodwins* Sands devouring,
Then the thicke-showr'd kisses here
Which now thy tyred lips must beare.
Such a harvest never was,
So rich and full of pleasure,

But 'tis spent as soone as reapt,
    So trustlesse is loves treasure.

Would it were dumb midnight now,
    When all the world lyes sleeping:
Would this place some Desert were,
    Which no man hath in keeping.
My desires should then be safe,
    And when you cry'd then would I laugh;
But if ought might breed offence,
    Love onely should be blamed:
I would live your servant still,
    And you my Saint unnamed.

♦ ♦ ♦ ♦ ♦

A secret love or two, I must confesse,
    I kindly welcome for change in close playing:
Yet my deare husband I love ne'erthelesse,
    His desires, whole or halfe, quickly allaying,
At all times ready to offer redresse.
    His owne he never wants, but hath it duely,
    Yet twits me, I keepe not touch with him truly.

The more a spring is drawne, the more it flowes;
    No Lampe lesse light retaines by lighting others:
Is hee a looser his losse that ne're knowes?
    Or is he wealthy that wast treasure smothers?
My churle vowes no man shall sent his sweet Rose:
    His owne enough and more I give him duely,
    Yet still he twits mee, I keepe not touch truly.

Wise Archers beare more then one shaft to field,
    The Venturer loads not with one ware his shipping:
Should Warriers learne but one weapon to weilde?
    Or thrive faire plants ere the worse for the slipping?
One dish cloyes, many fresh appetite yeeld:
    Mine owne Ile use, and his he shall have duely,
    Judge then what debter can keepe touch more truly.


◆ ◆ ◆ ◆ ◆


Her rosie cheekes, her ever smiling eyes,
Are Spheares and beds where Love in triumph lies:
Her rubine lips, when they their pearle unlocke,
Make them seeme as they did rise
All out of one smooth Currall Rocke.
Oh, that of other Creatures store I knew
More worthy, and more rare:
For these are old, and shee so new,
That her to them none should compare.

Oh, could she love, would shee but heare a friend,
Or that shee onely knew what sighs pretend.
Her lookes inflame, yet cold as Ice is shee.
Doe or speake, all's to one end,
For what shee is, that will shee be.
Yet will I never cease her prayse to sing,
Though she gives no regard:
For they that grace a worthlesse thing
Are onely greedy of reward.

♦ ♦ ♦ ♦ ♦

Where shall I refuge seeke, if you refuse mee?
In you my hope, in you my fortune lyes;
In you my life, though you unjust accuse me,
My service scorne, and merit underprise.
      Oh bitter griefe, that exile is become
      Reward for faith, and pittie deafe and dumbe.

Why should my firmnesse finde a seate so wav'ring?
My simple vowes, my love you entertain'd,
Without desert the same againe disfav'ring;
Yet I my word and passion hold unstain'd.
      Oh wretched me, that my chiefe joy should breede
      My onely griefe, and kindnesse pitty neede.


♦ ♦ ♦ ♦ ♦

Oft have I sigh'd for him that heares me not,
Who absent hath both love and mee forgot.
Oh yet I languish still through his delay:
Dayes seeme as yeares, when wisht friends breake their day.

Had hee but lov'd as common lovers use,
His faithlesse stay some kindnesse would excuse:
O yet I languish still, still constant mourne
For him that can breake vowes, but not returne.

Now let her change and spare not;
Since she proves strange I care not:
Fain'd love charm'd so my delight
That still I doted on her sight.
But she is gone, new joies imbracing
And my desires disgracing.

When did I erre in blindnesse?
Or vexe her with unkindnesse?
If my cares serv'd her alone,
Why is shee thus untimely gone?
True love abides to th' houre of dying;
False love is ever flying.

False, then farewell for ever:
Once false proves faithfull never.
Hee that boasts now of thy love
Shall soone my present fortunes prove:
Were he as faire as bright *Adonis,*
Faith is not had where none is.

♦ ♦ ♦ ♦ ♦

Were my hart as some mens are, thy errours would not move me:
But thy faults I curious finde, and speake because I love thee;
Patience is a thing divine and farre, I grant, above mee.

Foes sometimes befriend us more, our blacker deedes objecting,
Then th' obsequious bosome guest, with false respect affecting:
Friendship is the glasse of Truth, our hidden staines detecting.

While I use of eyes enjoy, and inward light of reason,
Thy observer will I be, and censor, but in season:
Hidden mischiefe to conceale in State and Love is treason.

♦ ♦ ♦ ♦ ♦

Maydes are simple, some men say:
They, forsooth, will trust no men.
But, should they mens wils obey,
Maides were very simple then.

Truth a rare flower now is growne,
Few men weare it in their hearts;
Lovers are more easily knowne
By their follies, then deserts.

Safer may we credit give
To a faithlesse wandring Jew
Then a young mans vowes beleeve
When he sweares his love is true.

Love they make a poore blinde childe,
But let none trust such as hee:
Rather then to be beguil'd,
Ever let me simple be.

♦ ♦ ♦ ♦ ♦

So tyr'd are all my thoughts, that sence and spirits faile;
Mourning I pine, and know not what I ayle.
O what can yeeld ease to a minde,
        Joy in nothing that can finde?

How are my powres fore-spoke? what strange distaste is this?
Hence, cruell hate of that which sweetest is:
Come, come delight, make my dull braine
    Feele once heate of joy againe.

The lovers teares are sweet, their mover makes them so;
Proud of a wound the bleeding Souldiers grow:
Poore I alone, dreaming, endure
    Griefe that knowes nor cause, nor cure.

And whence can all this grow? even from an idle minde,
That no delight in any good can finde.
Action alone makes the soule blest:
    Vertue dyes with too much rest.

♦ ♦ ♦ ♦ ♦

Why presumes thy pride on that, that must so private be
Scarce that it can good be cal'd, though it seemes best to thee,
Best of all that Nature fram'd, or curious eye can see?

Tis thy beauty, foolish Maid, that like a blossome growes,
Which who viewes no more enjoyes then on a bush a Rose;
That by manies handling fades, and thou art one of those.

If to one thou shalt prove true, and all beside reject,
Then art thou but one mans good, which yeelds a poore effect;
For the common'st good by farre deserves the best respect.

But if for this goodnesse thou thy selfe wilt common make,
Thou art then not good at all; so thou canst no way take
But to prove the meanest good, or else all good forsake.

Be not then of beauty proud, but so her colours beare
That they prove not staines to her that them for grace should weare:
So shalt thou to all more fayre then thou wert borne appeare.

♦ ♦ ♦ ♦ ♦

Kinde are her answeres,
    But her performance keeps no day,
Breaks time, as dancers
    From their own Musicke when they stray:
    All her free favors
And smooth words wing my hopes in vaine.
O did ever voice so sweet but only fain?
    Can true love yeeld such delay,
    Converting joy to pain?

Lost is our freedome
    When we submit to women so:
Why doe wee neede them,
    When in their best they worke our woe?
    There is no wisedome
Can alter ends by Fate prefixt:
O why is the good of man with evill mixt?
    Never were dayes yet cal'd two,
    But one night went betwixt.

♦ ♦ ♦ ♦ ♦

O griefe, O spight, to see poore Vertue scorn'd,
Truth far exil'd, False arte lov'd, Vice ador'd,
Free Justice sold, worst causes best adorn'd,
Right cast by Powre, Pittie in vaine implor'd!

O who in such an age could wish to live,
When none can have or hold, but such as give?

O times! O men! to Nature rebels growne,
Poore in desert, in name rich, proud of shame,
Wise but in ill: your stiles are not your owne,
Though dearely bought; honour is honest fame.
　　Old Stories onely goodnesse now containe,
　　And the true wisedome that is just, and plaine.

◆ ◆ ◆ ◆ ◆

O never to be moved,
　　O beauty unrelenting!
Hard hart, too dearely loved;
　　Fond love, too late repenting!
Why did I dreame of too much blisse?
Deceitfull hope was cause of this.
　　O heare mee speake this, and no more:
　　Live you in joy, while I my woes deplore.

All comforts despayred
　　Distaste your bitter scorning;
Great sorrowes unrepayred
　　Admit no meane in mourning:
Dye, wretch, since hope from thee is fled;
He that must dye is better dead.
　　O deare delight, yet, ere I dye,
　　Some pitty shew, though you reliefe deny.

♦ ♦ ♦ ♦ ♦

Breake now my heart and dye! Oh no, she may relent.
Let my despaire prevayle! Oh stay, hope is not spent.
Should she now fixe one smile on thee, where were despaire?
    The losse is but easie which smiles can repayre.
    A stranger would please thee, if she were as fayre.

Her must I love or none, so sweet none breathes as shee;
The more is my despayre, alas, shee loves not mee:
But cannot time make way for love through ribs of steele?
    The Grecian, inchanted all parts but the heele,
    At last a shaft daunted, which his hart did feele.

♦ ♦ ♦ ♦ ♦

Now winter nights enlarge
   The number of their houres,
And clouds their stormes discharge
   Upon the ayrie towres;
Let now the chimneys blaze
   And cups o'erflow with wine,
Let well-tun'd words amaze
   With harmonie divine.
Now yellow waxen lights
   Shall waite on hunny Love,
While youthfull Revels, Masks, and Courtly sights,
   Sleepes leaden spels remove.

This time doth well dispence
   With lovers long discourse;
Much speech hath some defence,
   Though beauty no remorse.

All doe not all things well:
    Some measures comely tread,
Some knotted Ridles tell,
    Some Poems smoothly read.
The Summer hath his joyes,
    And Winter his delights;
Though Love and all his pleasures are but toyes,
    They shorten tedious nights.

◆ ◆ ◆ ◆ ◆

Awake, thou spring of speaking grace, mute rest becomes not thee;
The fayrest women, while they sleepe, and Pictures equall bee.
        O come and dwell in loves discourses,
            Old renuing, new creating.
        The words which thy rich tongue discourses
            Are not of the common rating.

Thy voyce is as an Eccho cleare which Musicke doth beget,
Thy speech is as an Oracle which none can counterfeit:
        For thou alone, without offending,
            Hast obtain'd power of enchanting;
        And I could heare thee without ending,
            Other comfort never wanting.

Some little reason brutish lives with humane glory share;
But language is our proper grace, from which they sever'd are.
        As brutes in reason man surpasses,
            Men in speech excell each other:
        If speech be then the best of graces,
            Doe it not in slumber smother.

♦ ♦ ♦ ♦ ♦

What is it that all men possesse, among themselves conversing?
Wealth or fame, or some such boast, scarce worthy the rehearsing?
Women onely are mens good, with them in love conversing.

If weary, they prepare us rest; if sicke, their hand attends us;
When with griefe our hearts are prest, their comfort best befriends us:
Sweet or sowre, they willing goe to share what fortune sends us.

What pretty babes with paine they beare, our name and form presenting!
What we get, how wise they keepe, by sparing, wants preventing;
Sorting all their household cares to our observ'd contenting.

All this, of whose large use I sing, in two words is expressed:
Good wife is the good I praise, if by good men possessed;
Bad with bad in ill sute well, but good with good live blessed.

♦ ♦ ♦ ♦ ♦

Fire that must flame is with apt fuell fed,
Flowers that wil thrive in sunny soyle are bred;
How can a hart feele heate that no hope findes?
Or can hee love on whom no comfort shines?

Fayre, I confesse there's pleasure in your sight:
Sweet, you have powre, I grant, of all delight:
But what is all to mee, if I have none?
Churle that you are, t' injoy such wealth alone.

Prayers move the heav'ns, but finde no grace with you;
Yet in your lookes a heavenly forme I view:
Then will I pray againe, hoping to finde,
As well as in your lookes, heav'n in your minde.

Saint of my heart, Queene of my life, and love,
O let my vowes thy loving spirit move:
Let me no longer mourne through thy disdaine,
But with one touch of grace cure all my paine.

◆ ◆ ◆ ◆ ◆

If thou longst so much to learne (sweet boy) what 'tis to love,
Doe but fixe thy thought on mee, and thou shalt quickly prove.
    Little sute, at first, shal win
      Way to thy abasht desire,
    But then will I hedge thee in,
      Salamander-like, with fire.

With thee dance I will, and sing, and thy fond dalliance beare;
Wee the grovy hils will climbe, and play the wantons there;
    Other whiles wee'le gather flowres,
      Lying dalying on the grasse,
    And thus our delightfull howres
      Full of waking dreames shall passe.

When thy joyes were thus at height, my love should turne from thee;
Old acquaintance then should grow as strange as strange might be;
    Twenty rivals thou should'st finde
      Breaking all their hearts for mee,
    When to all Ile prove more kinde
      And more forward then to thee.

Thus thy silly youth, enrag'd, would soone my love defie;
But, alas, poore soule, too late: clipt wings can never flye.
    Those sweet houres which wee had past,
      Cal'd to minde, thy heart would burne;
    And, could'st thou flye ne'er so fast,
      They would make thee straight returne.

               ◆ ◆ ◆ ◆ ◆

    Shall I come, sweet Love, to thee,
      When the ev'ning beames are set?
    Shall I not excluded be?
      Will you finde no fained lett?
        Let me not, for pitty, more,
        Tell the long houres at your dore.

    Who can tell what theefe or foe,
      In the covert of the night,
  For his prey, will worke my woe,
      Or through wicked foule despight:
        So may I dye unredrest,
        Ere my long love be possest.

    But, to let such dangers passe,
      Which a lovers thoughts disdaine,
  'Tis enough in such a place
      To attend loves joyes in vaine.
        Doe not mocke me in thy bed,
        While these cold nights freeze me dead.

♦ ♦ ♦ ♦ ♦

Thrice tosse these Oaken ashes in the ayre,
Thrice sit thou mute in this inchanted chayre;
Then thrice three times tye up this true loves knot,
And murmur soft, shee will, or shee will not.

Goe burne these poys'nous weedes in yon blew fire,
These Screech-owles fethers, and this prickling bryer,
This Cypresse gathered at a dead mans grave:
That all thy feares and cares an end may have.

Then come, you Fayries, dance with me a round,
Melt her hard hart with your melodious sound.
In vaine are all the charmes I can devise:
She hath an Arte to breake them with her eyes.

♦ ♦ ♦ ♦ ♦

Fire, fire, fire, fire!
Loe here I burne in such desire
That all the teares that I can straine
Out of mine idle empty braine
Cannot allay my scorching paine.
Come *Trent,* and *Humber,* and fayre *Thames,*
Dread Ocean, haste with all thy streames:
And, if you cannot quench my fire,
O drowne both mee and my desire.

Fire, fire, fire, fire!
There is no hell to my desire:
See, all the Rivers backward flye,

And th' Ocean doth his waves deny,
For feare my heate should drinke them dry.
      Come, heav'nly showres, then, pouring downe;
      Come, you that once the world did drowne:
         Some then you spar'd, but now save all,
         That else must burne, and with mee fall.

♦ ♦ ♦ ♦ ♦

      Be thou then my beauty named,
Since thy will is to be mine:
      For by that am I enflamed,
Which on all alike doth shine.
         Others may the light admire,
         I onely truely feele the fire.

      But, if lofty titles move thee,
Challenge then a Sov'raignes place:
      Say I honour when I love thee,
Let me call thy kindnesse grace.
         State and Love things divers bee,
         Yet will we teach them to agree.

      Or, if this be not sufficing,
Be thou stil'd my Goddesse then:
      I will love thee sacrificing,
In thine honour Hymnes Ile pen.
         To be thine, what canst thou more?
         Ile love thee, serve thee, and adore.

◆ ◆ ◆ ◆ ◆

O sweet delight, O more then humane blisse,
With her to live that ever loving is;
To heare her speake, whose words so well are plac't,
That she by them, as they in her are grac't;
    Those lookes to view, that feast the viewers eye;
    How blest is he that may so live and dye!

Such love as this the golden times did know,
When all did reape, yet none tooke care to sow:
Such love as this an endlesse Summer makes,
And all distaste from fraile affection takes.
    So lov'd, so blest, in my belov'd am I;
    Which, till their eyes ake, let yron men envy.

◆ ◆ ◆ ◆ ◆

Thus I resolve, and time hath taught me so:
Since she is fayre and ever kinde to me,
Though she be wilde and wanton-like in shew,
Those little staines in youth I will not see.
    That she be constant, heav'n I oft implore;
    If pray'rs prevaile not, I can doe no more.

Palme tree the more you presse, the more it growes:
Leave it alone, it will not much exceede.
Free beauty if you strive to yoke, you lose,
And for affection strange distaste you breede.
    What Nature hath not taught, no Arte can frame:
    Wilde borne be wilde still, though by force made tame.

♦ ♦ ♦ ♦ ♦

Come, O come, my lifes delight,
Let me not in langour pine:
    Love loves no delay: thy sight,
The more enjoy'd, the more divine.
        O come, and take from mee
        The paine of being depriv'd of thee.

Thou all sweetnesse dost enclose,
Like a little world of blisse:
    Beauty guards thy lookes: the Rose
In them pure and eternall is.
        Come then, and make thy flight
        As swift to me as heav'nly light.

♦ ♦ ♦ ♦ ♦

Could my heart more tongues imploy
Then it harbors thoughts of griefe,
    It is now so farre from joy
That it scarce could aske reliefe.
        Truest hearts by deedes unkinde
        To despayre are most enclin'd.

Happy mindes, that can redeeme
Their engagements how they please,
    That no joyes or hopes esteeme
Halfe so pretious as their ease!
        Wisedome should prepare men so
        As if they did all foreknow.

Yet no Arte or Caution can
Growne affections easily change;
Use is such a Lord of Man
That he brookes worst what is strange.
Better never to be blest
Then to loose all at the best.

◆ ◆ ◆ ◆ ◆

Sleepe, angry beauty, sleep, and feare not me,
For who a sleeping Lyon dares provoke?
It shall suffice me here to sit and see
Those lips shut up that never kindely spoke.
What sight can more content a lovers minde
Then beauty seeming harmlesse, if not kinde?

My words have charm'd her, for secure shee sleepes,
Though guilty much of wrong done to my love;
And in her slumber, see! shee close-ey'd weepes!
Dreames often more then waking passions move.
Pleade, sleepe, my cause, and make her soft like thee,
That shee in peace may wake and pitty mee.

◆ ◆ ◆ ◆ ◆

Silly boy, 'tis ful Moone yet, thy night as day shines clearely;
Had thy youth but wit to feare, thou couldst not love so dearely.
Shortly wilt thou mourne when all thy pleasures are bereaved;
Little knowes he how to love that never was deceived.

This is thy first mayden flame, that triumphes yet unstayned;
All is artlesse now you speake, not one word yet is fayned;

All is heav'n that you behold, and all your thoughts are blessed:
But no Spring can want his Fall, each *Troylus* hath his *Cresseid.*

Thy well-order'd lockes ere long shall rudely hang neglected;
And thy lively pleasant cheare reade griefe on earth dejected.
Much then wilt thou blame thy Saint, that made thy heart so holy,
And with sighs confesse, in love, that too much faith is folly.

Yet, be just and constant still; Love may beget a wonder,
Not unlike a Summers frost, or Winters fatall thunder:
Hee that holds his Sweet-hart true unto his day of dying
Lives, of all that ever breath'd, most worthy the envying.

◆ ◆ ◆ ◆ ◆

Never love unlesse you can
Beare with all the faults of man:
Men sometimes will jealous bee
Though but little cause they see,
      And hang the head, as discontent,
      And speake what straight they will repent.

Men that but one Saint adore
Make a shew of love to more:
Beauty must be scorn'd in none,
Though but truely serv'd in one:
      For what is courtship, but disguise?
      True hearts may have dissembling eyes.

Men, when their affaires require,
Must a while themselves retire:
Sometimes hunt, and sometimes hawke,
And not ever sit and talke.

If these, and such like, you can beare,
Then like, and love, and never feare.

◆ ◆ ◆ ◆ ◆

So quicke, so hot, so mad is thy fond sute,
So rude, so tedious growne, in urging mee,
That faine I would with losse make thy tongue mute,
And yeeld some little grace to quiet thee:
 An houre with thee I care not to converse,
 For I would not be counted too perverse.

But roofes too hot would prove for men all fire,
And hils too high for my unused pace;
The grove is charg'd with thornes and the bold bryer;
Gray Snakes the meadowes shrowde in every place:
 A yellow Frog, alas, will fright me so,
 As I should start and tremble as I goe.

Since then I can on earth no fit roome finde,
In heaven I am resolv'd with you to meete;
Till then, for Hopes sweet sake, rest your tir'd minde,
And not so much as see mee in the streete:
 A heavenly meeting one day wee shall have,
 But never, as you dreame, in bed, or grave.

◆ ◆ ◆ ◆ ◆

Shall I then hope when faith is fled?
Can I seeke love when hope is gone?
Or can I live when Love is dead?
Poorely hee lives, that can love none.

Her vowes are broke, and I am free;
Shee lost her faith in loosing mee.

When I compare mine owne events,
When I weigh others like annoy,
    All doe but heape up discontents
That on a beauty build their joy.
        Thus I of all complaine, since shee
        All faith hath lost in loosing mee.

So my deare freedome have I gain'd
Through her unkindnesse and disgrace;
    Yet could I ever live enchain'd,
As shee my service did embrace.
        But shee is chang'd, and I am free:
        Faith failing her, Love dyed in mee.

◆ ◆ ◆ ◆ ◆

So sweet is thy discourse to me,
And so delightfull is thy sight,
    As I taste nothing right but thee.
O why invented Nature light?
        Was it alone for beauties sake,
        That her grac't words might better take?

No more can I old joyes recall:
They now to me become unknowne,
    Not seeming to have beene at all.
Alas, how soone is this love growne
        To such a spreading height in me
        As with it all must shadowed be!

♦ ♦ ♦ ♦ ♦

There is a Garden in her face,
Where Roses and white Lillies grow;
   A heav'nly paradice is that place,
Wherein all pleasant fruits doe flow.
   There Cherries grow, which none may buy
   Till Cherry ripe themselves doe cry.

Those Cherries fayrely doe enclose
Of Orient Pearle a double row,
   Which when her lovely laughter showes,
They looke like Rose-buds fill'd with snow.
   Yet them nor Peere nor Prince can buy,
   Till Cherry ripe themselves doe cry.

Her Eyes like Angels watch them still;
Her Browes like bended bowes doe stand,
   Threatning with piercing frownes to kill
All that attempt with eye or hand
   Those sacred Cherries to come nigh,
   Till Cherry ripe themselves doe cry.

♦ ♦ ♦ ♦ ♦

Young and simple though I am,
I have heard of *Cupids* name:
Guesse I can what thing it is
Men desire when they doe kisse.
   Smoake can never burne, they say,
   But the flames that follow may.

I am not so foule or fayre
To be proud, nor to despayre;
Yet my lips have oft observ'd,
Men that kisse them presse them hard,
   As glad lovers use to doe
   When their new met loves they wooe.

Faith, 'tis but a foolish minde,
Yet, me thinkes, a heate I finde,
Like thirst longing, that doth bide
Ever on my weaker side,
   Where they say my heart doth move.
   *Venus,* grant it be not love.

If it be, alas, what then?
Were not women made for men?
As good 'twere a thing were past,
That must needes be done at last.
   Roses that are over-blowne
   Growe lesse sweet, then fall alone.

Yet nor Churle, nor silken Gull
Shall my Mayden blossome pull:
Who shall not I soone can tell;
Who shall, would I could as well:
   This I know, who ere hee be,
   Love hee must, or flatter me.

♦ ♦ ♦ ♦ ♦

O Love, where are thy Shafts, thy Quiver, and thy Bow?
Shall my wounds onely weepe, and hee ungaged goe?
Be just, and strike him, to, that dares contemne thee so.

No eyes are like to thine, though men suppose thee blinde,
So fayre they levell when the marke they list to finde:
Then strike, o strike the heart that beares the cruell minde.

Is my fond sight deceived? or doe I *Cupid* spye
Close ayming at his breast, by whom despis'd I dye?
Shoot home, sweet *Love,* and wound him, that hee may not flye!

O then we both will sit in some unhaunted shade,
And heale each others wound which *Love* hath justly made:
O hope, o thought too vaine, how quickly dost thou fade!

At large he wanders still, his heart is free from paine,
While secret sighes I spend, and teares, but all in vaine:
Yet, *Love,* thou know'st, by right I should not thus complaine.

♦ ♦ ♦ ♦ ♦

Are you what your faire lookes expresse?
　　Oh then be kinde:
From law of Nature they digresse
　　Whose forme sutes not their minde:
　　Fairenesse seene in th' outward shape
　　Is but th' inward beauties Ape.

Eyes that of earth are mortall made,
　　What can they view?
All's but a colour or a shade,
　　And neyther alwayes true.
　　Reasons sight, that is eterne,
　　Ev'n the substance can discerne.

Soule is the Man; for who will so
    The body name?
And to that power all grace we owe
    That deckes our living frame.
    What, or how, had housen bin,
    But for them that dwell therein?

Love in the bosome is begot,
    Not in the eyes;
No beauty makes the eye more hot,
    Her flames the spright surprise:
    Let our loving mindes then meete,
    For pure meetings are most sweet.

♦ ♦ ♦ ♦ ♦

Beauty is but a painted hell:
        Aye me, aye me,
Shee wounds them that admire it,
Shee kils them that desire it.
        Give her pride but fuell,
        No fire is more cruell.

Pittie from ev'ry heart is fled,
        Aye me, aye me;
Since false desire could borrow
Teares of dissembled sorrow,
        Constant vowes turne truthlesse,
        Love cruell, Beauty ruthlesse.

Sorrow can laugh, and Fury sing,
        Aye me, aye me;
My raving griefes discover

I liv'd too true a lover:
   The first step to madnesse
   Is the excesse of sadnesse.

♦ ♦ ♦ ♦ ♦

Think'st thou to seduce me then with words that have no meaning?
Parats so can learne to prate, our speech by pieces gleaning:
Nurces teach their children so about the time of weaning.

Learne to speake first, then to wooe: to wooing much pertayneth:
Hee that courts us, wanting Arte, soone falters when he fayneth,
Lookes a-squint on his discourse, and smiles when hee complaineth.

Skilfull Anglers hide their hookes, fit baytes for every season;
But with crooked pins fish thou, as babes doe that want reason;
Gogions onely can be caught with such poore trickes of treason.

Ruth forgive me, if I err'd from humane hearts compassion
When I laught sometimes too much to see thy foolish fashion:
But, alas, who lesse could doe that found so good occasion?

♦ ♦ ♦ ♦ ♦

Her fayre inflaming eyes,
   Chiefe authors of my cares,
I prai'd in humblest wise
   With grace to view my teares:
      They beheld me broad awake,
      But, alasse, no ruth would take.

Her lips with kisses rich,
  And words of fayre delight,
I fayrely did beseech
  To pitty my sad plight:
    But a voyce from them brake forth
    As a whirle-winde from the North.

Then to her hands I fled,
  That can give heart and all;
To them I long did plead,
  And loud for pitty call:
    But, alas, they put mee off
    With a touch worse then a scoffe.

So backe I straight return'd,
  And at her breast I knock'd;
Where long in vaine I mourn'd,
  Her heart so fast was lock'd:
    Not a word could passage finde,
    For a Rocke inclos'd her minde.

Then downe my pray'rs made way
  To those most comely parts
That make her flye or stay,
  As they affect deserts:
    But her angry feete, thus mov'd,
    Fled with all the parts I lov'd.

Yet fled they not so fast
  As her enraged minde:
Still did I after haste,
  Still was I left behinde,
    Till I found 'twas to no end
    With a Spirit to contend.

◆ ◆ ◆ ◆ ◆

If any hath the heart to kill,
    Come rid me of this wofull paine.
For while I live I suffer still
    This cruell torment all in vaine:
        Yet none alive but one can guesse
        What is the cause of my distresse.

Thanks be to heav'n, no grievous smart,
    No maladies my limbes annoy;
I beare a sound and sprightfull heart,
    Yet live I quite depriv'd of joy:
        Since what I had, in vaine I crave,
        And what I had not, now I have.

A Love I had, so fayre, so sweet,
    As ever wanton eye did see.
Once by appointment wee did meete;
    Shee would, but ah, it would not be:
        She gave her heart, her hand shee gave;
        All did I give, shee nought could have.

What Hagge did then my powers forespeake,
    That never yet such taint did feele?
Now shee rejects me as one weake,
    Yet am I all compos'd of steele.
        Ah, this is it my heart doth grieve:
        Now though shee sees, shee'le not believe!

Beauty, since you so much desire
To know the place of *Cupids* fire:
About you somewhere doth it rest,
Yet never harbour'd in your brest,
Nor gout-like in your heele or toe;
What foole would seeke Loves flame so low?
But a little higher, but a little higher,
There, there, o there lyes *Cupids* fire.

Thinke not, when *Cupid* most you scorne,
Men judge that you of Ice were borne;
For, though you cast love at your heele,
His fury yet sometime you feele;
And where-abouts if you would know,
I tell you still, not in your toe:
But a little higher, but a little higher,
There, there, o there lyes *Cupids* fire.

♦ ♦ ♦ ♦ ♦

Faine would I wed a faire yong man that day and night could please mee,
When my mind or body grieved, that had the powre to ease mee.
Maids are full of longing thoughts that breed a bloudlesse sickenesse,
And that, oft I heare men say, is onely cur'd by quicknesse.
Oft have I beene woo'd and prai'd, but never could be moved:

Many for a day or so I have most dearely loved,
But this foolish mind of mine straight loaths the thing resolved.
If to love be sinne in mee, that sinne is soone absolved.
Sure, I thinke I shall at last flye to some holy Order;
When I once am setled there, then can I flye no farther.

Yet I would not dye a maid, because I had a mother:
As I was by one brought forth, I would bring forth another.

◆ ◆ ◆ ◆ ◆

Thrice tosse those oaken ashes in the ayer,
And thrice three tymes tye up this true-lovs Knott;
Thrice sitt you downe in this inchanted chaire
And murmure softe, *Shee will or shee will not.*
Goe burne those poysoned weeds in that blew fyre,
This *Cypres* gathered out a dead mans grave,
These *Scretchowles* fethers and the prickling bryer
That all thy Thornye cares an end may have.
Then come you *fairyes,* daunce with mee a round,
Daunce in a Circle, let my Love be Center.
Melodiously breath an inchanted sound,
Melt her hard harte, that some remorse may enter.
  In vayne are all the Charmes I can devise:
  She hath an arte to breake them with her eyes.

◆ ◆ ◆ ◆ ◆

Rose-cheekt *Lawra,* come,
Sing thou smoothly with thy beawties
Silent musick, either other
      Sweetely gracing.
  Lovely formes do flowe
From concent devinely framed;
Heav'n is musick, and thy beawties
      Birth is heavenly.
  These dull notes we sing
Discords neede for helps to grace them;

Only beawty purely loving
 Knowes no discord:
 But still mooves delight,
Like cleare springs renu'd by flowing,
Ever perfect, ever in them-
 selves eternall.

Lord haue mercy vpon mee, O heare my prayrs both

Lord haue mercy vpon mee, O heare my prayrs both

Lord haue mercy vpon mee, O heare my prayrs both

Lord haue mercy vpon mee, O heare my prayrs both

day and night, with teares pour'd forth to thee.

day and night, with teares pour'd forth to thee.

day and night, with teares pour'd forth to thee.

day and night, with teares pour'd forth to thee.

# About the Editor

❖❖

*Charles Simic's first volume of poetry was published in 1967, and many others have since followed. Two most recent ones are* Selected Poems: 1963–1983, *and* Unending Blues *in 1986. He has received awards from the Academy of American Poets, The National Institute of Arts and Letters and the Poetry Society of America. His other honors include a Guggenheim Foundation Fellowship, a Harriet Monroe Poetry Award, an Ingram Merrill Fellowship, and most recently a MacArthur Foundation Fellowship.*

*He has published numerous books of translations of Yugoslav poetry, and his own poetry has appeared in books, anthologies, and periodicals all over the world. His one book of essays is* The Uncertain Certainty *(The University of Michigan Press, 1985).*

*Mr. Simic is a Professor of English at the University of New Hampshire, where he teaches American Literature and Creative Writing.*